MOTORCYCLES

MARYSA STORM

BLACK
RABBIT
BOOKS

Bolt Jr. is published by Black Rabbit Books
P.O. Box 3263, Mankato, Minnesota, 56002.
www.blackrabbitbooks.com
Copyright © 2020 Black Rabbit Books

Michael Sellner, designer; Omay Ayres, photo researcher

Names: Storm, Marysa, author.
Title: Motorcycles / by Marysa Storm.
Description: Mankato, Minnesota : Black Rabbit Books,
[2020] | Series: Bolt Jr. Wild rides | Includes bibliographical
references and index. | Audience: Age 6-8. | Audience:
Grades K to 3.
Identifiers: LCCN 2019002809 (print) | LCCN 2019004052
(ebook) | ISBN 9781623101954 (e-book) |
ISBN 9781623101893 (library binding) |
ISBN 9781644661215 (paperback)
Subjects: LCSH: Motorcycles–Juvenile literature.
Classification: LCC TL440.15 (ebook) | LCC TL440.15 .S76
2020 (print) | DDC 629.227/5–dc23
LC record available at https://lccn.loc.gov/2019002809

Printed in the United States. 5/19

Image Credits

automobiles.honda.com: Honda Motor Company, 7; iStock: Bill
Oxford, 22–23; Hirkophoto, 10–11; powersports.honda.com: Honda
Powersports, 6–7; rideapart.com: Ride Apart, 21; Shutterstock:
AHMAD FAIZAL YAHYA, Cover; Alexander Kirch, 10; Corinna Huter, 13;
Creative icon styles, 14; grafixx, 3, 24; Jag_cz, 16–17; Master1305,
20–21; mooinblack, 18–19; NarayTrace, 8–9; tarczas, 12;
yamahamotorsports.com: Yamaha Motor Sports, 1, 4, 5

Contents

A Wild Ride

A motorcycle waits at a red light. The rider **revs** the engine. The light changes, and she takes off. The bike roars. It's soon out of sight.

rev: to cause an engine to run more quickly

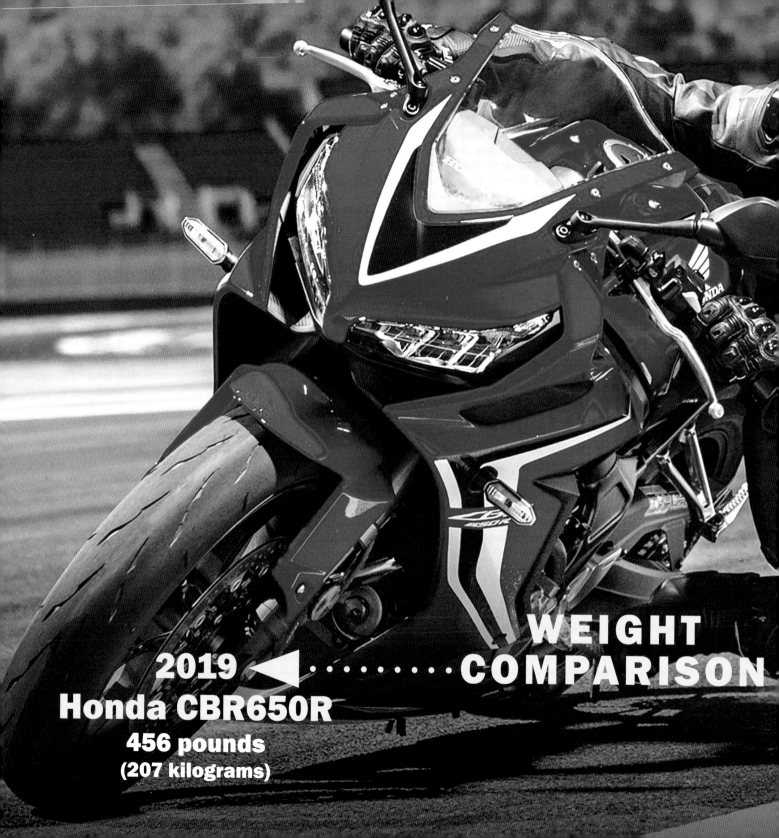

WEIGHT COMPARISON

2019 ◄ ·········
Honda CBR650R
456 pounds
(207 kilograms)

Fast and Light

Motorcycles are small vehicles. They have two wheels and a motor. They're lighter than cars. They hit top speeds faster. Some people use them for road trips. Others race them.

▶ **2019 Honda Accord LX**
3,131 pounds
(1,420 kg)

Motorcycle

exhaust pipes

engine

frame

throttle

tires

9

CHAPTER 2

Different Types

There are many kinds of motorcycles.
Riders sit in **relaxed** positions on
standard bikes. Cruisers are even more
comfortable. They have wide seats.
Riders use them for long trips.

relaxed: comfortable

Sport and Dirt Bikes

Sport bikes have high seats. They're built for speed. Dirt bikes have tough frames. They have **knobby** tires. People ride them on bumpy trails.

knobby: having bumps

Popular Motorcycle Companies

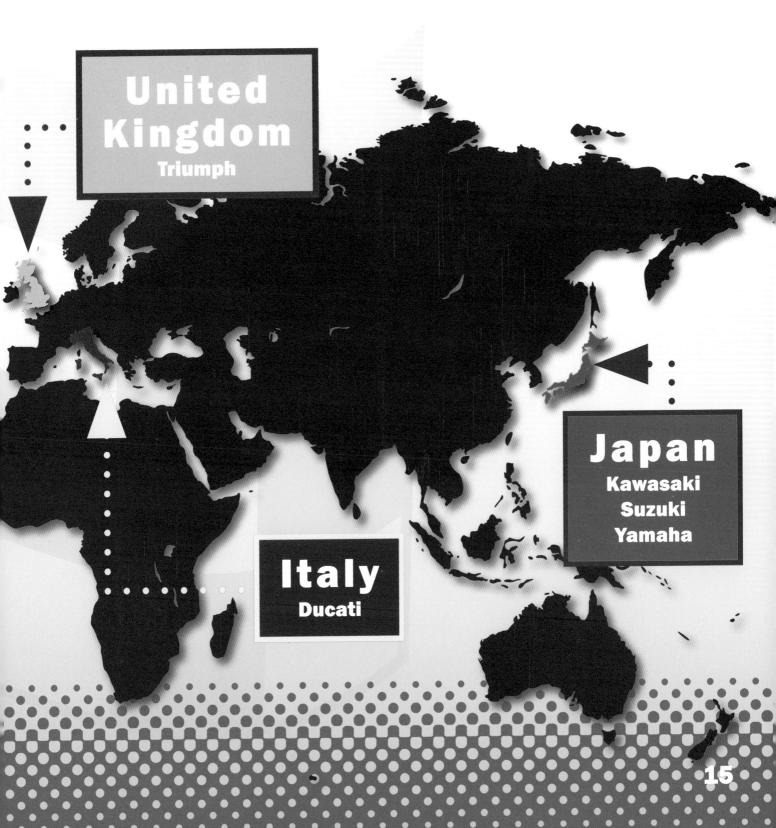

United Kingdom
Triumph

Japan
Kawasaki
Suzuki
Yamaha

Italy
Ducati

Racing On

Motorcycles have been around for years. People first made them in the 1800s. They soon became popular. People everywhere started riding them.

FACT

Soldiers around the world use motorcycles during wars.

The Future

Over the years, motorcycles have changed. People use new materials to make them. Some have electric motors. One thing has stayed the same, though. People love riding them.

Staying Safe

Helmets keep riders safe. Many states have laws that say people must wear them.

Bonus Facts

People can do **tricks** on bikes.

Jackets also keep riders safe.

Motorcycles use less gas than cars.

Many riders customize their bikes.

customize: to change in order to fit the needs of a person

21

READ MORE/WEBSITES

Bowman, Chris. *Motorcycles.* Mighty Machines in Action. Minneapolis: Bellwether Media, Inc., 2018.

Dieker, Wendy Strobel. *Motorcycles.* Mighty Machines. Mankato, MN: Amicus, 2020.

Hoefler, Kate. *Rabbit and the Motorbike.* San Francisco: Chronicle Books LLC, 2019.

A Brief History of Motorcycles
www.bikersbasics.com/history-of-motorcycles/

Motorcycle
kids.britannica.com/kids/article/motorcycle/400135

Motorcycle Facts for Kids
kids.kiddle.co/Motorcycle

GLOSSARY

customize (KUHS-tuh-mahyz)—to change in order to fit the needs of a person

knobby (NOB-ee)—having bumps

relaxed (ree-LAKSD)—comfortable

rev (REV)—to cause an engine to run more quickly